THE NAMES OF GOD

FOLAKE HASSAN

The Righteous Publishing House

London UK

Copyright © Folake Hassan 2014

Unless otherwise stated all Scripture quotations are taken from The Amplified Bible (AMP)

All rights reserved. No part of this publication may be reproduced or transmitted in any form or by any means, electronic or mechanical, including photocopying, recording, or by any informative storage and retrieval system, without the written permission of the Author.

The Names of God

Published by The Righteous Publishing House

Flat 7, 93 Villiers Road

Willesden. London NW2 5QB

Visit Our Website at:

www.theblessedchristian.co.uk

Appreciation

I give all praises to God Almighty, who chose me and qualified me to be a carrier of His Anointing, a carrier of His Presence. I thank God for enduing me with His Wisdom. My sincere appreciation also goes to the men and women from every part of the world that God has used to minister His Words to bless me. I thank my children for their good attitudes that have enabled me to walk a good walk in my journey as a Christian. I thank my parents for nurturing and taking good care of me through my childhood and they still do today.

Table of Contents

Introduction 1
The Names of God 13
Becoming a Christian 66

Introduction

In every tradition, culture and nationality, there is something about Name. The name of a person, cities or a thing signifies and represents the personalities or attributes of that person. A name at times signifies what a person can do and/or what they cannot do. Names at times may mean what we want something or a person to become or manifest.

The first assignment God gave to Adam was to give names to all creatures and whatever Adam called every living creature that was its name. (Genesis 2: 19-20)

The Bible teaches us that "the power of life and of death is in the tongue" what we constantly call a thing or anyone is what they are likely to become. **My Prayer is that The Lord will empower us to decree His Goodness in The Name of Jesus Christ.**

What you constantly call God is what he will become in your life; for example if we believe that God is a good God; what we will eventually receive from God will be Gods goodness. It is good to know who God is; to acknowledge what He has done for us and what He is capable of bringing to pass in our lives.

In the Book of Psalm 91:14-15 of the Bible, the Lord promises to deliver and set on high those who know His Name. He said He will answer us; He will be with us in times of trouble; He will deliver us and honour us. With long life will He satisfy us and show us His Salvation because we know His Name i.e. we know His attributes, we know who He is, we know what He is capable of doing; because of this He promised to save us.

Because he has set his love upon Me, therefore will I deliver him; I will set him on high, <u>because he knows and understands My name</u> [has a personal knowledge of My mercy, love, and kindness—trusts and relies on Me, knowing I will never forsake him, no, never]. He shall call upon Me, <u>and I will answer him; I will be with him in trouble, I will deliver him and</u> honour him. With long life will I satisfy him and show him My salvation. (Psalm 91: 14-16)

Instances from the Bible

Several instances in the Bible; the names of people were changed to reflect better personalities:

   a. Abram was changed to Abraham: (Genesis 17:5)

   b. Sarai was changed to Sarah: (Genesis 17:15)

   c. Jacob was changed to Israel: (Genesis 32:28)

   d. Jabez prayed to God to bless him; he was given the name Jabez by his mother which means sorrow simply because she bored him in sorrow: (1 Chronicles 4:9-10) though Jabez did not changed his name, but He prayed to God so that the meaning of his name will not manifest in his life.

The Lord God promises great deliverance for those who love Him; for those who know Him personally.

Knowing and understanding the Name of The Lord means we have a personal knowledge of God's mercy, love and kindness; it means we know who God is. It means we trust and relies on Him knowing He will never forsake us.

The Lord God promises to answer us if we continue calling His Name; if we acquaint ourselves with what His Names means.

I pray that our focus will be on the faithfulness of God always and not on the challenges and unnecessary distractions that surrounds us.

To see the manifestations of the powers of God; we must be willing to discover who God is and continue to call Him by His Name especially during our Praise and Worship and at regular intervals as we have the opportunities; and at the same time we must remember not to call the Name of the Lord in vain; each time we call His Name we must believe that He will manifest what that Name stands for.

We must all develop a habit and the attitude of calling God, stop calling your problems, stop meditating on your challenges, stop dwelling on the pains you are going through, start building a good relationship with God from today by getting to know Who He is by calling Him regularly, especially in your praise and fellowship with Him. Meditate regularly on the personalities of God; and that is what He will manifest in your life. I pray that the Holy Spirit will encourage each and every one of us and teach us to discover more of who God is.

Calling God regularly by His Name especially during our praise and worships will help us to release glory and the presence of God into our environment; The Lord God inhabits the praises of His People (Psalm 22:3).

Therefore My people shall know <u>what My name is</u> and what it means; therefore they shall know in that day that I am He who speaks; behold, I AM! (Isaiah 52: 6)

Oh, that You would rend the heavens and that You would come down, that the mountains might quake and flow down at Your presence— As when fire kindles the brushwood and the fire causes the waters to boil—<u>to make Your name known to Your adversaries</u>, that the nations may tremble at Your presence! (Isaiah 64: 1 & 2)

Therefore [says the Lord] behold, I will make them know—[yes] this once I will make them know My power and My might; and they will know and recognize that <u>My name is the Lord</u>. (Jeremiah 16:21)

If the Name of The Lord is the only thing you know it will work for you, if all your trust is only on God; the Name of God will answer for you.

<u>Meditate on The Words of God so that Your Lips may Confess it and not Problems that Surrounds You.</u>

Listen (consent and submit) to the words of the wise, and apply your mind to my knowledge; For it will be pleasant if you keep them in your mind [believing them]; <u>your lips will be accustomed to [confessing] them</u>. So that your trust (belief, reliance, support, and confidence) may be in the Lord, I have made known these things to you today, even to you. (Proverbs 22: 17-19)

Confess and meditate on The Word of God in the face of any challenges. Do not fear what satan may be whispering to you, confess the faithfulness of God until your good result manifest and even after, continue and allow your joy to overflow. Look for The Name of The Lord that matches your challenges and start meditating on it rather than your negative or the unpleasant situations.

Choose to dwell on The Word of God. For instance:

To avoid worries about any situations, start by practising to meditate on The Name of The Lord as Your Jehovah Shalom i.e. God is Your **Prince of Peace:**

For to us a Child is born, to us a Son is given; and the government shall be upon His shoulder, and His name shall be called Wonderful Counselor, Mighty God, Everlasting Father [of Eternity], **Prince of Peace**. (Isaiah 9:6) That is Who God is.

….may grace (spiritual blessing) and **peace** be given you in increasing abundance [**that spiritual**

peace to be realized in and through Christ, freedom from fears, agitating passions, and moral conflicts]. (1 Peter 1:2b)

For all Good Things You Need, you can start to confess God as Your Jehovah-Jireh meaning that God is Your **Provider** (See Genesis 22: 8 &14)

As Christians, we should develop the habit of training our children to develop the habit of Trusting in The Lord for All Good Things in The Name of Jesus Christ.

Example from The Bible: God called Moses so as to send him to help delivered the Israelites from their taskmaster, called Pharaoh; Moses was worried and ask God; what should he says to the Israelites that will make them truly believe that God has sent him, the answer God gave him was that if Moses mentioned to The Israelites **the Name of The Lord**, the Israelites will believe Moses as the true servant of the Most High God:

> **And Moses said to God, Behold, when I come to the Israelites and say to them, The God of your fathers has sent me to you, and they say to me, What is His name? What shall I say to them? And God said to Moses, I AM WHO I AM and WHAT I AM, and I WILL BE WHAT I WILL BE; and He said, You shall say this to the Israelites: I AM has sent me to you! God said also to**

Moses, This shall you say to the Israelites: The Lord, the God of your fathers, of Abraham, of Isaac, and of Jacob, has sent me to you! This is My name forever, and by this name I am to be remembered to all generations. (Exodus 3: 11-15)

Why The Name of The Lord?

1. And it shall be that whoever shall call upon the Name of the Lord [invoking, adoring, and worshiping the Lord—Christ] shall be saved. (Acts 2: 21)

2. And whoever shall call on the Name of the Lord shall be delivered and saved, for in Mount Zion and in Jerusalem there shall be those who escape, as the Lord has said, and among the remnant [of survivors] shall be those whom the Lord calls. (Joel 2: 32)

3. For everyone who calls upon the name of the Lord [invoking Him as Lord] will be saved. (Romans 10:13)

4. O give thanks unto the Lord, call upon His name, make known His doings among the peoples! Sing to Him, sing praises to Him; meditate on and talk of all His marvellous deeds and devoutly praise them. Glory in His holy name; let the hearts of those rejoice who seek and require the Lord [as their indispensable necessity]. Seek, inquire of and for the Lord, and crave Him and His strength (His might and inflexibility to temptation); seek and require His face and His presence [continually] evermore. [Earnestly] remember the marvellous deeds that He has done, His miracles and wonders, the

judgments and sentences which He pronounced [upon His enemies, as in Egypt]. (Psalm 105: 1-5)

5. Blessed is he who comes in the Name of the Lord; we bless you from the house of the Lord [you who come into His sanctuary under His guardianship]. (Psalm 118:26)

6. I have [earnestly] remembered Your Name, O Lord, in the night, and I have observed Your law. (Psalm 119:55)

7. And when that time comes, you will ask nothing of Me [you will need to ask Me no questions]. I assure you, most solemnly I tell you, that My Father will grant you whatever you ask in My Name [as presenting all that I Am]. (John 16:23) **(Also see The NKJV Translation)**

8. Up to this time you have not asked a [single] thing in My Name [as presenting all that I Am]; but now ask and keep on asking and you will receive, so that your joy (gladness, delight) may be full and complete. (John 16:24)

9. Enter into His gates with thanksgiving and a thank offering and into His courts with praise! Be thankful and say so to Him, bless and affectionately praise His name! (Psalm 100:4)

10. Blessed be the name of the Lord from this time forth and forever. From the rising of the sun to the

going down of it and from east to west, the name of the Lord is to be praised! (Psalm 113:2-3)

11. And those who went before and those who followed cried out [with a cry of happiness], Hosanna! [Be graciously inclined and propitious to Him!] Praised and blessed is He Who comes in the name of the Lord! Praised and blessed in the name of the Lord is the coming kingdom of our father David! Hosanna (O save us) in the highest [heaven]! (Mark 11: 9-10)

We Should Manifest the Personalities of God

The day we accept and confess Jesus Christ as our Lord and Saviour was the day we moved from death to life; that was the day our personalities supposed to start changing to align with that of God. We were created in God's image; therefore what we should manifest in our live time and after should be the personalities and the attributes of God.

As we continue to find out who God is; I pray that we will all be transformed to be created in God's Image and manifest Gods personality in The Name of Jesus Christ.

Learn to process, meditate; think; swallow and digest the Word of God regularly. Whatever we think about constantly tends to happens sometimes in our lives. We must not think evil; we should always have Godly thoughts in The Name of Jesus Christ.

Looking through this book will deliver into you the answers to questions and challenges you may be facing at a particular time as you choose to believe and meditate on each of God's Name.

THE NAMES OF GOD AS INDICATED IN THE BIBLE

The Almighty God : When Abram was ninety-nine years old, the Lord appeared to him and said, I am the Almighty God; walk and live habitually before Me and be perfect (blameless, wholehearted, complete).(Genesis 17:1)

The Amen: So [it shall be] that he who invokes a blessing on himself in the land shall do so by saying, May the God of truth and fidelity [the Amen] bless me; and he who takes an oath in the land shall swear by the God of truth and faithfulness to His promises [the Amen], because the former troubles are forgotten and because they are hidden from My eyes. (Isaiah 65:16)

God Almighty: I appeared to Abraham, to Isaac, and to Jacob as God Almighty [El-Shaddai], but by My name the Lord [Yahweh—the redemptive name of God] I did not make Myself known to them [in acts and great miracles]. (Exodus 6:3)

God The Father: Who were chosen and foreknown by God the Father and consecrated (sanctified, made holy) by the Spirit to be obedient to Jesus Christ (the Messiah) and to be sprinkled with [His] blood: May grace (spiritual blessing) and peace be given you in increasing abundance [that spiritual peace to be realized in and through Christ, freedom from fears, agitating passions, and moral conflicts]. (1 Peter 1:2)

The Almighty: I am the Alpha and the Omega, the Beginning and the End, says the Lord God, He Who is and Who was and Who is to come, the Almighty (the Ruler of all). (Revelation 1:8)

Alpha and Omega: I am the Alpha and the Omega, the Beginning and the End, says the Lord God, He Who is and Who was and Who is to come, the Almighty (the Ruler of all). (Revelation 1:8)

Advocate: But when the Comforter (Counsellor, Helper, Advocate, Intercessor, Strengthener, Standby) comes, Whom I will send to you from the Father, the Spirit of Truth Who comes (proceeds) from the Father, He [Himself] will testify regarding Me. (John 15: 26)

My little children, I write you these things so that you may not violate God's law and sin. But if anyone should sin, we have an Advocate (One Who will intercede for us) with the Father—[it is] Jesus Christ [the all] righteous [upright, just, Who conforms to the Father's will in every purpose, thought, and action]. (1 John 2: 2)

The Ancient of Days: I kept looking until thrones were placed [for the assessors with the Judge], and the Ancient of Days [God, the eternal Father] took His seat, Whose garment was white as snow and the hair of His head like pure wool. His throne was like the fiery flame; its wheels were burning fire. (Daniel 7:9)

I saw in the night visions, and behold, on the clouds of the heavens came one like a Son of man, and He came to the Ancient of Days and was presented before Him. (Daniel 7:13)

Until the Ancient of Days came, and judgment was given to the saints of the Most High [God], and the time came when the saints possessed the kingdom. (Daniel 7:22)

The Anointed One: So that [the genuineness] of your faith may be tested, [your faith] which is infinitely more precious than the perishable gold which is tested and purified by fire. [This proving of your faith is intended] to redound to [your] praise and glory and honour when Jesus Christ (the Messiah, the Anointed One) is revealed. (! Peter 1:7)

Our Arm: O Lord, be gracious to us; we have waited [expectantly] for You. Be the arm [of Your servants—their strength and defense] every morning, our salvation in the time of trouble. (Isaiah 33:2)

The Author of Salvation: And He has raised up a Horn of salvation [a mighty and valiant Helper, the Author of salvation] for us in the house of David His servant (Luke 1: 69)

The Beginning: He also is the Head of [His] body, the church; seeing He is the Beginning, the Firstborn from among the dead, so that He alone in everything and in every respect might occupy the chief place [stand first and be preeminent]. (Colossians 1:18)

The Beginning and the End: I am the Alpha and the Omega, the Beginning and the End, says the Lord God, He Who is and Who was and Who is to come, the Almighty (the Ruler of all). (Revelation 1:8)

Blessed: His name shall endure forever; His name shall continue as long as the sun [indeed, His name continues before the sun]. And men shall be blessed and bless themselves by Him; all nations shall call Him blessed! Blessed be the Lord God, the God of Israel, Who alone does wondrous things! Blessed be His glorious name forever; let the whole earth be filled with His glory! Amen and Amen! (Psalm 72: 17-19) also see Psalm 68: 19 & 35.

The Bread of Life: I am the Bread of Life [that gives life—the Living Bread]. (John 6: 48)

Our Buckler: [Then] He will cover you with His pinions, and under His wings shall you trust and find refuge; His truth and His faithfulness are a shield and a buckler. (Proverbs 91:4)

Our Creator: For from Him and through Him and to Him are all things. [For all things originate with Him and come from Him; all things live through Him, and all things centre in and tend to consummate and to end in Him.] To Him be glory forever! Amen (so be it). (Romans 11:36)

For it was in Him that all things were created, in heaven and on earth, things seen and things unseen, whether thrones, dominions, rulers, or authorities; all things were created and exist through Him [by His service, intervention] and in and for Him (Colossians 1:16)

Prayer: I pray that from today the fresh anointing, the fresh abilities and the creative abilities of God will fill each and every one of us in The Name of Jesus Christ. The Lord God will empower us to start creating and manifesting Godly purposes in The Name of Jesus Christ. He will fill us with Godly ideas and Wisdom to be the true replica of Him by starting to build our nations; by starting to create all we needs as God gives us the abilities and the Wisdom in The Name of Jesus Christ.

Note: It is good news for us to know that all good and perfects gifts comes from our Lord and Saviour. This assures us that we will have all our needs met by God as long as we avail ourselves of the grace to listen and obey His instructions. I pray that the Lord will give to each and every one of us, a discerning heart to hear Him and to obey in The Name of Jesus Christ.

Also there is hope for us that The Father God will bring to maturity all that concerns us. He will bring us to the state of perfections through His Spirits that dwell in us. He will bring us to the level of Honours we deserve in Christ in The Name of Jesus Christ. An Excellent spirit will manifest in us and through us in the Name of Jesus Christ. We will not remain or die as Baby Christians in the Name of Jesus Christ. We will rise to positions of Honours and the right levels of maturity in The Name of Jesus Christ.

For more passages where God is referred to as a Creator in the Bible see: Isaiah 43:15; Isaiah 40:28; Romans 1:25; Job 41:10;

Ecclesiastes 12:1; Ecclesiastes 12:6; Job 41:34; Hebrews 13:7

Jesus Christ: And this is eternal life: [it means] to know (to perceive, recognize, become acquainted with, and understand) You, the only true and real God, and [likewise] to know Him, Jesus [as the] Christ (the Anointed One, the Messiah), Whom You have sent. (John 17: 3)

She will bear a Son, and you shall call His name Jesus [the Greek form of the Hebrew Joshua, which means Saviour], for He will save His people from their sins [that is, prevent them from failing and missing the true end and scope of life, which is God]. (Matthew 1:21)

The name 'Jesus' in the Bible actually means, a Saviour; a Deliverer

It is a thing of joy, healing, hope and strength to be assured that all who call on The Name of the Lord shall be saved from their sins. It is something of gladness to discover that sins will not have dominion over us because Jesus Christ came to pay the price on our behalf. It is a joy to find out that we will not miss our purpose in life. I thank God for Jesus Christ Who came to give life a meaning. I thank God for Jesus who came to act as intermediaries between humanity and God. He came to reconcile man to God.

Also see: 2 Timothy 1:1; 1 Timothy 1.1; Galatians 3:26; 1 Corinthians 16:23; Titus 3:6; Acts 15:26

Comforter: But when the Comforter (Counselor, Helper, Advocate, Intercessor, Strengthener, Standby) comes, Whom I will send to you from the Father, the Spirit of Truth Who comes (proceeds) from the Father, He [Himself] will testify regarding Me. (John 15: 26)

The Chief Cornerstone: For thus it stands in Scripture: Behold, I am laying in Zion a chosen (honoured), precious chief Cornerstone, and he who believes in Him [who adheres to, trusts in, and relies on Him] shall never be disappointed or put to shame. (1 Peter 2: 6)

The Chief Shepherd: And [then] when the <u>Chief Shepherd</u> is revealed, you will win the conqueror's crown of glory. (1 Peter 5:4)

Counsellor: But when the Comforter (<u>Counselor</u>, Helper, Advocate, Intercessor, Strengthener, Standby) comes, Whom I will send to you from the Father, the Spirit of Truth Who comes (proceeds) from the Father, He [Himself] will testify regarding Me. (John 15: 26)

Our Confidant: By fearful and glorious things [that terrify the wicked but make the godly sing praises] do You answer us in righteousness (rightness and justice), O God of our salvation, <u>You Who are the confidence</u> and hope of all the ends of the earth and of those far off on the seas. (Psalm 65:5)

Our Confidence: <u>For the Lord shall be your confidence</u>, firm and strong, and shall keep your foot from being caught [in a trap or some hidden danger]. (Proverbs 3:26)

Our Consecration: But it is from Him that you have your life in Christ Jesus, Whom God made our Wisdom from God, [revealed to us a knowledge of the divine plan of salvation previously hidden, manifesting itself as] our Righteousness [thus making us upright and putting us in right standing with God], and our Consecration [making us pure and holy], and our Redemption [providing our ransom from eternal penalty for sin]. (1 Corinthians 1: 30)

Our Covenant Keeper: My covenant will I not break or profane, nor alter the thing that is gone out of My lips (Psalm 89:34)

The Creator and Ruler of all Things: Remember your leaders and superiors in authority [for it was they] who brought to you the Word of God. Observe attentively and consider their manner of living (the outcome of their well-spent lives) and imitate their faith (their conviction that God exists and is the Creator and Ruler of all things, the Provider and Bestower of eternal salvation through Christ, and their leaning of the entire human personality on God in absolute trust and confidence in His power, wisdom, and goodness). (Hebrews 13: 7)

The Creator of the ends of The Earth: Have you not known? Have you not heard? The everlasting God, the Lord, the Creator of the ends of the earth, does not faint or grow weary; there is no searching of His understanding. (Isaiah 40:28)

The Creator of Israel: I am the Lord, your Holy One, the Creator of Israel, your King. (Isaiah 43:15)

My Defence: He only is my Rock and my Salvation, my Defense and my Fortress, I shall not be greatly moved. (Psalm 62: 2) also see Isaiah 33:2

Our Defence: But let all those who take refuge and put their trust in You rejoice; let them ever sing and shout for joy, because <u>You make a covering over them and defend them</u>; let those also who love Your name be joyful in You and be in high spirits. (Psalm 5:11)

A God of Deliverance and Salvation: <u>God is to us a God of deliverances and salvation</u>; and to God the Lord belongs escape from death [setting us free]. ((Psalm 68:20) **see Psalm 118:21 as well.**

The Door: So Jesus said again, I assure you, most solemnly I tell you, that I Myself am <u>the Door for the sheep</u>. John 10:7)

El-Shaddai: I appeared to Abraham, to Isaac, and to Jacob as God Almighty <u>[El-Shaddai]</u>, but by My name the Lord [Yahweh—the redemptive name of God] I did not make Myself known to them [in acts and great miracles]. (Exodus 6:3)

Emmanuel: Behold, the virgin shall become pregnant and give birth to a Son, and they shall call His name <u>Emmanuel</u>—which, when translated, means, God with us. (Matthew 1: 23)

Eternal: [Just as] You have granted Him power and authority over all flesh (all humankind), [now glorify Him] <u>so that He may give eternal life to all whom You have given Him. And this is eternal life: [it means] to know (to perceive, recognize, become acquainted with, and understand) You</u>, the only true and real God, and [likewise] to know Him, Jesus [as the] Christ (the Anointed One, the Messiah), Whom You have sent. (John 17: 2 & 3)

The Ever Living One: And the Ever-living One [I am living in the eternity of the eternities]. I died, but see, I am alive forevermore; and I possess the keys of death and Hades (the realm of the dead). (Revelation 1:18)

Everlasting Father: For to us a Child is born, to us a Son is given; and the government shall be upon His shoulder, and His name shall be called Wonderful Counsellor, Mighty God, Everlasting Father [of Eternity], Prince of Peace. (Isaiah 9:6)

The Everlasting God: Have you not known? Have you not heard? The everlasting God, the Lord, the Creator of the ends of the earth, does not faint or grow weary; there is no searching of His understanding. (Isaiah 40:28)

The Everlasting Rock: So trust in the Lord (commit yourself to Him, lean on Him, hope confidently in Him) forever; for the Lord God is an everlasting Rock [the Rock of Ages]. (Isaiah 26:4)

The Everlasting Strength: Trust ye in the LORD for ever: for in the LORD JEHOVAH is everlasting strength (Isaiah 26: 4) KJV

The Exalted: And in that day you will say, Give thanks to the Lord, call upon His name and by means of His name [in solemn entreaty]; declare and make known His deeds among the peoples of the earth, proclaim that His name is exalted! (Isaiah 12:4)

Excellent in Wisdom: This also comes from the Lord of hosts, Who is wonderful in counsel [and] excellent in wisdom and effectual working. (Isaiah 28:29)

Our Father: Pray, therefore, like this: Our Father Who is in heaven, hallowed (kept holy) be Your name (Matthew 6:9)

The Father Who Judges All: And if you call upon Him as [your] Father Who judges each one impartially according to what he does, [then] you should conduct yourselves with true reverence throughout the time of your temporary residence [on the earth, whether long or short]. (1 Peter 1: 17)

A Father of the Fatherless: A father of the fatherless and a judge and protector of the widows is God in His holy habitation. (Psalm 68: 5)

Faithful: Yet the Lord is faithful, and He will strengthen [you] and set you on a firm foundation and guard you from the evil [one]. (2 Thessalonians 3:3)

The Finisher of Our Faith: Looking away [from all that will distract] to Jesus, Who is the Leader and the Source of our faith [giving the first incentive for our belief] and is also it's <u>Finisher [bringing it to maturity and perfection]</u>. He, for the joy [of obtaining the prize] that was set before Him, endured the cross, despising and ignoring the shame, and is now seated at the right hand of the throne of God. (Hebrew 12:2)

The First and The Last: When I saw Him, I fell at His feet as if dead. But He laid His right hand on me and said, do not be afraid<u>! I am the First and the Last</u>, (Revelation 1:17)

Thus says the Lord, the King of Israel and his Redeemer, the Lord of hosts: <u>I am the First and I am the Last</u>; besides Me there is no God. (Isaiah 44:6)

The Firstborn of all Creation: [Now] He is the exact likeness of the unseen God [the visible representation of the invisible]; He is the Firstborn of all creation. (Colossians 1:15)

The Firstborn from Among the Dead: He also is the Head of [His] body, the church; seeing He is the Beginning, <u>the Firstborn from among the dead</u>, so that He alone in everything and in every respect might occupy the chief place [stand first and be preeminent]. (Colossians 1:18)

The Firstborn of the Dead: And from Jesus Christ the faithful and trustworthy Witness, the Firstborn of the dead [first to be brought back to life] and the Prince (Ruler) of the kings of the earth. To Him Who ever loves us and has once [for all] loosed and freed us from our sins by His own blood, (Revelation 1:5)

My Fortress: He only is my Rock and my Salvation, my Defense and my Fortress, I shall not be greatly moved. (Psalm 62: 2)

The Lord of hosts is with us; the God of Jacob is our Refuge (our Fortress and High Tower) (Psalm 46:7).

God: Sing to God, sing praises to His name, cast up a highway for Him Who rides through the deserts—His name is the Lord—be in high spirits and glory before Him! (Psalm 68: 4)

The God of Abraham, Isaac and Jacob: God said also to Moses, This shall you say to the Israelites: The Lord, the God of your fathers, of Abraham, of Isaac, and of Jacob, has sent me to you! This is My name forever, and by this name I am to be remembered to all generations. (Exodus 3: 15)

The God of The Whole Earth: For your Maker is your Husband—the Lord of hosts is His name—and the Holy One of Israel is your Redeemer; the God of the whole earth He is called. (Isaiah 54:5)

God With Us: Behold, the virgin shall become pregnant and give birth to a Son, and they shall call His name Emmanuel—which, when translated, means, God with us. (Matthew 1: 23)

The Great: Great is our Lord and of great power; His understanding is inexhaustible and boundless. (Psalm 147: 5)

The Great I Am: Great is our Lord and of great power; His understanding is inexhaustible and boundless. (Psalm 147: 5)

And God said to Moses, I AM WHO I AM *and* WHAT I AM, *and* I WILL BE WHAT I WILL BE; and He said, You shall say this to the Israelites: I AM has sent me to you! (Exodus 3:14)

Guardian: Blessed is he who comes in the name of the Lord; we bless you from the house of the Lord [you who come into His sanctuary under His guardianship]. (Psalm 118:26)

Our Guide: But when He, the Spirit of Truth (the Truth-giving Spirit) comes, He will guide you into all the Truth (the whole, full Truth). For He will not speak His own message [on His own authority]; but He will tell whatever He hears [from the Father; He will give the message that has been given to Him], and He will announce and declare to you the things that are to come [that will happen in the future]. (John 16:13)

The Head of The Body meaning The Head of the Church: He also is the Head of [His] body, the church; seeing He is the Beginning, the Firstborn from among the dead, so that He alone in everything and in every respect might occupy the chief place [stand first and be preeminent]. (Colossians 1:18) **Also see: Ephesians 1: 22-23**

The Head of all Rule, Principalities and Powers: And you are in Him, made full and having come to fullness of life [in Christ you too are filled with the Godhead—Father, Son and Holy Spirit—and reach full spiritual stature]. And He is the Head of all rules and authority [of every angelic principality and power]. (Colossians 2:10)

Our Healer: "He sends forth His word and heals them and rescues them from the pit and destruction" (Psalm 107:20)

He personally bore our sins in His [own] body on the tree [as on an altar and offered Himself on it], that we might die (cease to exist) to sin and live to righteousness. By His wounds you have been healed. (1 Peter 2: 24)

My Helper: But when the Comforter (Counsellor, Helper, Advocate, Intercessor, Strengthener, Standby) comes, Whom I will send to you from the Father, the Spirit of Truth Who comes (proceeds) from the Father, He [Himself] will testify regarding Me. (John 15: 26)

So we take comfort and are encouraged and confidently and boldly say, The Lord is my Helper; I will not be seized with alarm [I will not fear or dread or be terrified]. What can man do to me? (Hebrews 13:6)

The Help of My Countenance: Why are you cast down, O my inner self? And why should you moan over me and be disquieted within me? Hope in God and wait expectantly for Him, for I shall yet praise Him, Who is the help of my countenance, and my God. (Psalm 42:11)

He Who is and Who Was and Who is to Come: I am the Alpha and the Omega, the Beginning and the End, says the Lord God, He Who is and Who was and Who is to come, the Almighty (the Ruler of all). (Revelation 1: 8)

The High and Lofty One: For thus says the high and lofty One—He Who inhabits eternity, Whose name is Holy: I dwell in the high and holy place, but with him also who is of a thoroughly penitent and humble spirit, to revive the spirit of the humble and to revive the heart of the thoroughly penitent [bruised with sorrow for sin]. (Isaiah 57:15)

He Who Inhabits The Eternity: For thus says the high and lofty One—He Who inhabits eternity, Whose name is Holy: I dwell in the high and holy place, but with him also who is of a thoroughly penitent and humble spirit, to revive the spirit of the humble and to revive the heart of the thoroughly penitent [bruised with sorrow for sin]. (Isaiah 57:15)

Holy: The Lord of hosts—<u>regard Him as holy</u> and honour <u>His holy name</u> [by regarding Him as your only hope of safety], and let Him be your fear and let Him be your dread [lest you offend Him by your fear of man and distrust of Him]. (Isaiah 8:13)

The Holy One of Israel: For your Maker is your Husband—the Lord of hosts is His name—and <u>the Holy One of Israel</u> is your Redeemer; the God of the whole earth He is called. (Isaiah 54:5) **also see Isaiah 29:19**

The Holy One: I am the Lord, <u>your Holy One</u>, the Creator of Israel, your King (Isaiah 43:15)

The Holy Ghost: But the Comforter, which is <u>the Holy Ghost</u>, whom the Father will send in my name, he shall teach you all things, and bring all things to your remembrance, whatsoever I have said unto you. (John 14: 26) **KJV**

The Lord of Hosts: Who is [He then] this King of glory? <u>The Lord of hosts</u>, He is the King of glory. (Psalm 24: 10)

<u>The Lord of hosts</u> is with us; the God of Jacob is our Refuge (our Fortress and High Tower). (Psalm 46:7)

Hope: By fearful and glorious things [that terrify the wicked but make the godly sing praises] do You answer us in righteousness (rightness and justice), O God of our salvation, You Who are the confidence and hope of all the ends of the earth and of those far off on the seas. (Psalm 65:5)

The Hope of All the Earth: By fearful and glorious things [that terrify the wicked but make the godly sing praises] do You answer us in righteousness (rightness and justice), O God of our salvation, You Who are the confidence and hope of all the ends of the earth and of those far off on the seas. (Psalm 65:5)

My Husband: For your Maker is your Husband—the Lord of hosts is His name—and the Holy One of Israel is your Redeemer; the God of the whole earth He is called. (Isaiah 54:5)

I Am Who I Am (I am That I am: KJV): And God said to Moses, I AM WHO I AM and WHAT I AM, and I WILL BE WHAT I WILL BE; and He said, You shall say this to the Israelites: I AM has sent me to you! (Exodus 3: 14)

I Am: And God said to Moses, I AM WHO I AM and WHAT I AM, and I WILL BE WHAT I WILL BE; and He said, You shall say this to the Israelites: I AM has sent me to you! (Exodus 3: 14)

Intercessor: But when the Comforter (Counselor, Helper, Advocate, Intercessor, Strengthener,

Standby) comes, Whom I will send to you from the Father, the Spirit of Truth Who comes (proceeds) from the Father, He [Himself] will testify regarding Me. (John 15: 26)

My Firm Impenetrable Rock: Let the words of my mouth and the meditation of my heart be acceptable in Your sight, O Lord, my [firm, impenetrable] Rock and my Redeemer. (Psalm 19:14)

Mighty and Impenetrable to Temptation: God is our Refuge and Strength [mighty and impenetrable to temptation], a very present and well-proved help in trouble. (Psalm 46: 1)

Immortal: [It is that purpose and grace] which He now has made known and has fully disclosed and made real [to us] through the appearing of our Savior Christ Jesus, Who annulled death and made it of no effect and brought life and immortality (immunity from eternal death) to light through the Gospel. (2 Timothy 1:10)

The Invincible God: The Lord God is my Strength, my personal bravery, and my invincible army; He makes my feet like hinds' feet and will make me to walk [not to stand still in terror, but to walk] and make [spiritual] progress upon my high places [of trouble, suffering, or responsibility]! (Habakkuk 3:19)

Jehovah: Trust ye in the LORD for ever: for in the LORD JEHOVAH is everlasting strength (Isaiah 26:4)

That men may know that thou, whose name alone is JEHOVAH, art the most high over all the earth (Psalm 83:18)

Behold, God is my salvation; I will trust, and not be afraid: for the LORD JEHOVAH is my strength and my song; he also is become my salvation (Isaiah 12:2) **KJV**

Jehovah-nissi: (Our Victory): And Moses built an altar, and called the name of it Jehovah nissi. For he said, because the LORD hath sworn that the LORD will have war with Amalek from generation to generation. (Exodus 17:15-16)**KJV**

Note: My Victory is sure and it is permanent in Christ, evil shall no longer attends to me, evil shall not attend to the readers of this book and all our loved ones in The Name of Jesus Christ. For the Lord God will have war with anything that has been fighting us and our families for generations, ignorance, death, sickness, pain, poverty, sadness and grieves shall not have rooms in our lives in The Name of Jesus Christ.

Jehovah Shalom: (Our Peace) and the LORD said unto him, Peace be unto thee; fear not: thou shalt not die. Then Gideon built an altar there unto the LORD, and called it Jehovah shalom: unto this day it is yet in Ophrah of the Abiezrites. (Judges 6:23-24) **KJV**

Jehovah-jireh: (Our Provider) And Abraham lifted up his eyes, and looked, and behold behind him a ram caught in a thicket by his horns: and Abraham went and took the ram, and offered him up for a burnt offering in the stead of his son. And Abraham called the name of that place Jehovah-jireh: as it is said to this day, in the mount of the LORD it shall be seen. (Genesis 22:13-14) **KJV**

Note: Thank You Lord God for providing for all our needs; thank You for our lives will no longer be the sacrifice but the Lamb You provided. Jesus Christ is our sacrifice, no human lives or that of our flocks shall ever be the price again. We will live to enjoy the blessings of The Lord to the full in the land of the living in The Name of Jesus Christ.

Jehovah-Shammah: (The Lord is Present) It was round about eighteen thousand measures: and the name of the city from that day shall be, The LORD is there. (Ezekiel 48:35) **KJV**

My Joy: Then [Ezra] told them, Go your way, eat the fat, drink the sweet drink, and send portions to him for whom nothing is prepared; for this day is holy to our Lord. And be not grieved and depressed, for the joy of the Lord is your strength and stronghold. (Nehemiah 8:10)

Also that day they offered great sacrifices and rejoiced, for God had made them rejoice with great joy; the women also and the children rejoiced. The joy of Jerusalem was heard even afar off. (Nehemiah 12:43)

A Judge and The Protector of the Widows: A father of the fatherless and a judge and protector of the widows is God in His holy habitation. (Psalm 68: 5)

The Most High Judge: And if you call upon Him as [your] Father Who judges each one impartially according to what he does, [then] you should conduct yourselves with true reverence throughout the time of your temporary residence [on the earth, whether long or short]. (1 Peter 1: 17)

Our Judge: For the Lord is our Judge, the Lord is our Lawgiver, the Lord is our King; He will save us. (Isaiah 33:22)

Our King: For the Lord is our Judge, the Lord is our Lawgiver, the Lord is our King; He will save us. (Isaiah 33:22) also see Isaiah 43:15

King of Glory: Lift up your heads, O you gates; and be lifted up, you age-abiding doors, that the King of glory may come in. (Psalm 24:7)

King of kings: And on His garment (robe) and on His thigh He has a name (title) inscribed, KING OF KINGS AND LORD OF LORDS (REVELATION 19:16)

The Lord: Have you not known? Have you not heard? The everlasting God, the Lord, the Creator of the ends of the earth, does not faint or grow weary; there is no searching of His understanding. (Isaiah 40:28)

Our Lawgiver: For the Lord is our Judge, the Lord is our Lawgiver, the Lord is our King; He will save us. (Isaiah 33: 22)

The Lord my Saviour: Happy are you, O Israel, and blessing is yours! Who is like you, a people saved by the Lord, the Shield of your help, the Sword that exalts you! Your enemies shall come fawning and cringing, and submit feigned obedience to you, and you shall march on their high places," (Deuteronomy 33:29)

Also: 2 Samuel 22.4; Psalm 18:3;Psalm 34:6; Isaiah 45:22; Psalm 44:7; Psalm 116:6

The Lamb of God: The next day John saw Jesus coming to him and said, Look! There is the Lamb of God, Who takes away the sin of the world. (John 1:29)

Our Leader: Looking away [from all that will distract] to Jesus, <u>Who is the Leader</u> and the Source of our faith [giving the first incentive for our belief] and is also it's Finisher [bringing it to maturity and perfection]. He, for the joy [of obtaining the prize] that was set before Him, endured the cross, despising and ignoring the shame, and is now seated at the right hand of the throne of God. (Hebrew 12:2)

The Lord: Sing to God, sing praises to His name, cast up a highway for Him Who rides through the deserts—<u>His name is the Lord</u>—be in high spirits and glory before Him! (Psalm 68:4)

LORD OF LORDS: And on His garment (robe) and on His thigh He has a name (title) inscribed, KING OF KINGS AND <u>LORD OF LORDS</u> (REVELATION 19:16)

The Lord God Who Rides Through the Deserts: Sing to God, sing praises to His name, <u>cast up a highway for Him Who rides through the deserts</u>— His name is the Lord—be in high spirits *and* glory before Him! (Psalm 68: 4)

The Lord God Who Gives The Solitary <u>Families</u>: <u>God places the solitary in families</u> and gives the desolate a home in which to dwell; He leads the prisoners out to prosperity; but the rebellious dwell in a parched land. (Psalm 68:6)

<u>Note:</u>

This particular verse of the Bible shows that God hate loneliness, God is not the Author of any unnecessary solitary situations, hence God made it possible for people to have family, for no one to live on their own.

I pray that we will always be in support of what God initiated by willing to have a Good God glorifying family in The Name of Jesus Christ.

The Lord Is A God Of Justice: And therefore the Lord [earnestly] waits [expecting, looking, and longing] to be gracious to you; and therefore He lifts Himself up, that He may have mercy on you and show loving-kindness to you. For the Lord is a God of justice. Blessed (happy, fortunate, to be envied) are all those who [earnestly] wait for Him, who expect and look and long for Him [for His victory, His favour, His love, His peace, His joy, and His matchless, unbroken companionship]! (Isaiah 30:18)

The Lord Gives A Desolate A Home To Dwell: God places the solitary in families and gives the desolate a home in which to dwell; He leads the prisoners out to prosperity; but the rebellious dwell in a parched land. (Psalm 68:6)

Note:

This should be good news for us that The Lord God will always provide Shelter for His people. It is the desire of The Lord for each and every one of us to have a place called Home.

The Lord Leads The Prisoners Out To Prosperity: God places the solitary in families and gives the desolate a home in which to dwell; He leads the prisoners out to prosperity; but the rebellious dwell in a parched land. (Psalm 68:6)

The Last One: For I know that my Redeemer and Vindicator lives, and at last He [the Last One] will stand upon the earth (Job 19:25)

The Life: Jesus said to him, I am the Way and the Truth and the Life; no one comes to the Father except by (through) Me. (John 14:6)

In Him was Life, and the Life was the Light of men. (John 1: 4)

My Light: The Lord is my Light and my Salvation—whom shall I fear or dread? The Lord is the Refuge and Stronghold of my life—of whom shall I be afraid? (Psalm 27:1)

Our Light: And the Light shines on in the darkness, for the darkness has never overpowered it [put it out or absorbed it or appropriated it, and is unreceptive to it]. (John 1: 5)

And this is the message [the message of promise] which we have heard from Him and now are reporting to you: <u>God is Light</u>, and there is no darkness in Him at all [no, not in any way]. (1 John 1: 5)

The Lion of Judah: Then one of the elders [of the heavenly Sanhedrin] said to me, stop weeping! See, <u>the Lion of the tribe of Judah</u>, the Root (Source) of David, has won (has overcome and conquered)! He can open the scroll and break its seven seals! (Revelation 5:5)

The Living Stone: Come to Him [then, to that] <u>Living Stone</u> which men tried and threw away, but which is chosen [and] precious in God's sight. (1 Peter 2: 4)

The Living Water: But whoever takes a drink of the <u>water</u> that I will give him shall never, no never, be thirsty any more…… (John 4:14a)

For My people have committed two evils: they have forsaken Me, <u>the Fountain of living waters</u>….. (Jeremiah 2: 13)

Love: And we know (understand, recognize, and are conscious of, by observation and by experience) and believe (adhere to and put faith in and rely on) the love God cherishes for us. <u>God is love</u>, and he who dwells and continues in love dwells and continues in God, and God dwells and continues in him. (1 John 4:16)

My Maker: For your Maker is your Husband—the Lord of hosts is His name—and the Holy One of Israel is your Redeemer; the God of the whole earth He is called. (Isaiah 54:5)

Our Maker: Woe to him who strives with his Maker!—a worthless piece of broken pottery among other pieces equally worthless [and yet presuming to strive with his Maker]! Shall the clay say to him who fashions it, what do you think you are making? Or, your work has no handles? (Isaiah 45:9)

Master: And you must not be called masters (leaders), for you have one Master (Leader), the Christ. (Matthew 23:10)

The Mediator of A Better Covenant: But as it now is, He [Christ] has acquired a [priestly] ministry which is as much superior and more excellent [than the old] as the covenant (the agreement) of which He is the Mediator (the Arbiter, Agent) is superior and more excellent, [because] it is enacted and rests upon more important (sublimer, higher, and nobler) promises. (Hebrews 8:6)

The Most High Judge: I said, You are gods [since you judge on My behalf, as My representatives]; indeed, all of you are children of the Most High (Psalm 82:6)

The Merciful and Gracious God: The Lord is merciful and gracious, slow to anger and plenteous in mercy and loving-kindness. (Psalm 103:8)

Messiah: For to you is born this day in the town of David a Saviour, Who is Christ (the Messiah) the Lord! (Luke 2:11)

Mighty God: For to us a Child is born, to us a Son is given; and the government shall be upon His shoulder, and His name shall be called Wonderful Counsellor, Mighty God, Everlasting Father [of Eternity], Prince of Peace. (Isaiah 9:6)

The Mighty One of Jacob: How he swore to the Lord and vowed to the Mighty One of Jacob (Psalm 132:2)

A Miracle Worker: This, the first of His signs (miracles, wonderworks), Jesus performed in Cana of Galilee, and manifested His glory [by it He displayed His greatness and His power openly], and His disciples believed in Him [adhered to, trusted in, and relied on Him]. (John 2:11)

The Most High God: He who dwells in the secret place of the Most High shall remain stable and fixed under the shadow of the Almighty [Whose power no foe can withstand]. (Psalm 91:1)

Offer to God the sacrifice of thanksgiving, and pay your vows to the Most High. (Psalm 50:14)

For when God made [His] promise to Abraham, He swore by Himself, since <u>He had no one greater by whom to swear</u> (Hebrews 6:13)

Also see: Psalm 73:11; Psalm 78:35; Daniel 4:2; Psalm 78:56; Genesis 14:20; Daniel 7:18; Psalm 46:4; Psalm 57:2; Luke 1:32; Psalm 82:6; Daniel 7:22.

The Lord Mighty in Battle: Who is the King of glory? The Lord strong and mighty, the <u>Lord mighty in battle</u>. (Psalm 24:8)

Omnipotent: I saw no temple in the city, for the Lord God <u>Omnipotent</u> [Himself] and the Lamb [Himself] are its temple.(Revelation 21:22)

And [from] the altar I heard [the] cry, Yes, Lord God the <u>Omnipotent,</u> Your judgments (sentences, decisions) are true and just and righteous!(Revelation 16;7)

Exclaiming, To You we give thanks, Lord God <u>Omnipotent</u>, [the One] Who is and [ever] was, for assuming the high sovereignty and the great power that are Yours and for beginning to reign.(Revelation 11:17)

Also see Isaiah 14:26

Omniscient: Then you will understand the reverent and worshipful fear of the Lord and find the knowledge of [our omniscient] God. (Proverbs 2:5) **see Proverbs 15:11; See Psalm 147:5**

Omnipresent: God is our Refuge and Strength [mighty and impenetrable to temptation], a very present and well-proved help in trouble. (Psalm 46:1)

From His dwelling place He looks [intently] upon all the inhabitants of the earth (Psalm 33:14)

Can anyone hide himself in secret places so that I cannot see him? says the Lord. Do not I fill heaven and earth? says the Lord. (Jeremiah 23:24)

And the Ever-living One [I am living in the eternity of the eternities]. I died, but see, I am alive forevermore; and I possess the keys of death and Hades (the realm of the dead). (Revelation 1:18)

The One Who Called Us: But as the One Who called you is holy, you yourselves also be holy in all your conduct and manner of living. (1 Peter 1:15)

Our Peace: Peace I leave with you; My [own] peace I now give and bequeath to you. Not as the world gives do I give to you. Do not let your hearts be troubled, neither let them be afraid. [Stop allowing yourselves to be agitated and disturbed; and do not permit yourselves to be fearful and intimidated and cowardly and unsettled.] (John 14:27)

Our Perfection: The Lord will perfect that which concerns me; Your mercy and loving-kindness, O Lord, endure forever—forsake not the works of Your own hands.(Psalm 138:8)

The Power of God: But to those who are called, whether Jew or Greek (Gentile), Christ [is] the Power of God and the Wisdom of God. (1 Corinthians 1: 24)

A Very Present Help in Trouble: God is our Refuge and Strength [mighty and impenetrable to temptation], a very present and well-proved help in trouble. (Psalm 46: 1)

The Precious Cornerstone: Therefore thus says the Lord God, Behold, I am laying in Zion for a foundation a Stone, a tested Stone, a precious Cornerstone of sure foundation; he who believes (trusts in, relies on, and adheres to that Stone) will not be ashamed or give way or hasten away [in sudden panic]. (Isaiah 28: 16)

The Preeminent: He also is the Head of [His] body, the church; seeing He is the Beginning, the Firstborn from among the dead, so that He alone in everything and in every respect might occupy the chief place [stand first and be preeminent]. (Colossians 1:18)

Prince of Peace: For to us a Child is born, to us a Son is given; and the government shall be upon His shoulder, and His name shall be called Wonderful

Counsellor, Mighty God, Everlasting Father [of Eternity], <u>Prince of Peace.</u> (Isaiah 9:6)

The Prince (Ruler) of The Kings of The Earth: And from Jesus Christ the faithful and trustworthy Witness, the Firstborn of the dead [first to be brought back to life] and <u>the Prince (Ruler) of the kings of the earth</u>. To Him Who ever loves us and has once [for all] loosed and freed us from our sins by His own blood, (Revelation 1:5)

The Provider and The Bestower of Eternal Salvation: Remember your leaders and superiors in authority [for it was they] who brought to you the Word of God. Observe attentively and consider their manner of living (the outcome of their well-spent lives) and imitate their faith (their conviction that God exists and is the Creator and Ruler of all things, <u>the Provider and Bestower of eternal salvation through Christ</u>, and their leaning of the entire human personality on God in absolute trust and confidence in His power, wisdom, and goodness). (Hebrews 13:7)

Our Provider: Abraham said, My son, <u>God Himself will provide</u> a lamb for the burnt offering. So the two went on together (Genesis 22:8)

Our Redeemer: For I know that my <u>Redeemer</u> and Vindicator lives, and at last He [the Last One] will stand upon the earth" (Job 19:25)

"Into Your hands I commit my spirit; <u>You have redeemed me,</u> O Lord, the God of truth and faithfulness. (Psalm 31:5)

Our Redemption: But it is from Him that you have your life in Christ Jesus, Whom God made our Wisdom from God, [revealed to us a knowledge of the divine plan of salvation previously hidden, manifesting itself as] our Righteousness [thus making us upright and putting us in right standing with God], and our Consecration [making us pure and holy], and <u>our Redemption [providing our ransom from eternal penalty for sin]</u>. (1 Corinthians 1:30)

My Refuge: The Lord is my Light and my Salvation—whom shall I fear or dread? The Lord is the <u>Refuge</u> and Stronghold of my life—of whom shall I be afraid? (Psalm 27:1)

Our Refuge and Strength: <u>God is our Refuge and Strength</u> [mighty and impenetrable to temptation], a very present and well-proved help in trouble. (Psalm 46:1)

The Resurrection and Life: Jesus said to her, <u>I am [Myself] the Resurrection and the Life</u>. Whoever believes in (adheres to, trusts in, and relies on) Me, although he may die, yet he shall live (John 11:25)

Our Righteousness: But it is from Him that you have your life in Christ Jesus, Whom God made our

Wisdom from God, [revealed to us a knowledge of the divine plan of salvation previously hidden, manifesting itself as] <u>our Righteousness</u> [<u>thus making us upright and putting us in right standing with God</u>], and our Consecration [making us pure and holy], and our Redemption [providing our ransom from eternal penalty for sin]. (1 Corinthians 1: 30)

The Righteous Judge: And will not [<u>our just</u>] <u>God</u> defend and protect and avenge His elect (His chosen ones), who cry to Him day and night? Will He defer them and delay help on their behalf? (Luke 18:7)

The Righteous One: And he said, The God of our forefathers has destined and appointed you to come progressively to know His will [to perceive, to recognize more strongly and clearly, and to become better and more intimately acquainted with His will], and to see <u>the Righteous One</u> (Jesus Christ, the Messiah), and to hear a voice from His [own] mouth and a message from His [own] lips; (Acts 22:14)

The Root of David: Then one of the elders [of the heavenly Sanhedrin] said to me, stop weeping! See, the Lion of the tribe of Judah<u>, the Root (Source) of David</u>, has won (has overcome and conquered)! He can open the scroll and break its seven seals! (Revelation 5:5)

Our Rock: "There is none holy like the Lord, there is none besides You; there is no Rock like our God" (1 Samuel 2:2)

My Rock and My Salvation: He only is my Rock and my Salvation, my Defense and my Fortress, I shall not be greatly moved. (Psalm 62:2)

The Rock of Ages: So trust in the Lord (commit yourself to Him, lean on Him, hope confidently in Him) forever; for the Lord God is an everlasting Rock [the Rock of Ages]. (Isaiah 26:4)

Rock of Offence: And, A Stone that will cause stumbling and a Rock that will give [men] offense; they stumble because they disobey and disbelieve [God's] Word, as those [who reject Him] were destined (appointed) to do. (1 Peter 2: 8)

The Ruler of All: I am the Alpha and the Omega, the Beginning and the End, says the Lord God, He Who is and Who was and Who is to come, the Almighty (the Ruler of all). (Revelation 1:8)

My Salvation: The Lord is my Light and my Salvation—whom shall I fear or dread? The Lord is the Refuge and Stronghold of my life—of whom shall I be afraid? (Psalm 27:1) also see Isaiah 12:2

Our Sanctuary: And He shall be a sanctuary [a sacred and indestructible asylum to those who reverently fear and trust in Him]; but He shall be a Stone of stumbling and a Rock of offense to both the houses of Israel, a trap and a snare to the inhabitants of Jerusalem. (Isaiah 8:14)

Saviour: For to you is born this day in the town of David <u>a Saviour</u>, Who is Christ (the Messiah) the Lord! (Luke 2:11)

Our Shield and Buckler: [Then] He will cover you with His pinions, and under His wings shall you trust and find refuge; <u>His truth *and* His faithfulness are a shield and a buckler</u>. (Psalm 91:4)

The Shield of My Help: Happy are you, O Israel, and blessing is yours! Who is like you, a people saved by the Lord, <u>the Shield of your help</u>, the Sword that exalts you! Your enemies shall come fawning and cringing, and submit feigned obedience to you, and you shall march on their high places (Deuteronomy 33:29)

The Sword That Exalts Me: Happy are you, O Israel, and blessing is yours! Who is like you, a people saved by the Lord, the Shield of your help, <u>the Sword that exalts you</u>! Your enemies shall come fawning and cringing, and submit feigned obedience to you, and you shall march on their high places" (Deuteronomy 33:29)

My Salvation: The Lord is my Light and my Salvation—whom shall I fear or dread? The Lord is the Refuge and Stronghold of my life—of whom shall I be afraid? (Psalm 27:1)

The God Of Our Salvation: By fearful and glorious things [that terrify the wicked but make the godly sing praises] do You answer us in righteousness (rightness and justice), O God of our salvation, You Who are the confidence and hope of all the ends of the earth and of those far off on the seas (Psalm 65: 5)

Our Shepherd: The Lord is my Shepherd [to feed, guide, and shield me], I shall not lack (Psalm 23:1)

Son of God: And I have seen [that happen—I actually did see it] and my testimony is that this is the Son of God! (John 1: 34)

My Song: Behold, God is my salvation; I will trust, and not be afraid: for the LORD JEHOVAH is my strength and my song; he also is become my salvation. (Isaiah 12:2) **KJV**

The Sovereign God: For who has known the mind of the Lord and who has understood His thoughts, or who has [ever] been His counsellor? (Romans 11:34)

The Sovereign Ruler: And you shall know that I am the Lord [your Sovereign Ruler], when I have opened your graves and caused you to come up out of your graves, O My people (Ezekiel 37:13)

The Source Of Our Faith: Looking away [from all that will distract] to Jesus, Who is the Leader and the Source of our faith [giving the first incentive for our belief] and is also its Finisher [bringing it to maturity and perfection]. He, for the joy [of obtaining the prize] that was set before Him, endured the cross, despising and ignoring the shame, and is now seated at the right hand of the throne of God. (Hebrew 12:2)

Yet for us there is [only] one God, the Father, Who is the **Source** of all things and for Whom we [have life], and one Lord, Jesus Christ, through and by Whom are all things and through and by Whom we [ourselves exist]. (1 Corinthians 8:6)

My Stronghold: The Lord is my Light and my Salvation—whom shall I fear or dread? The Lord is the Refuge and Stronghold of my life—of whom shall I be afraid? (Psalm 27:1)

Our Stronghold: The Lord of hosts is with us; the God of Jacob is our Refuge (our High Tower and Stronghold). (Psalm 46:11)

A Sure Foundation: Therefore thus says the Lord God, Behold, I am laying in Zion for a foundation a Stone, a tested Stone, a precious Cornerstone of sure foundation; he who believes (trusts in, relies on, and adheres to that Stone) will not be ashamed or give way or hasten away [in sudden panic]. (Isaiah 28:16)

The Lord Strong and Mighty: Who is the King of glory? The Lord strong and mighty, the Lord mighty in battle. (Psalm 24: 8)

The Lord Our Righteousness: In His days Judah shall be saved and Israel shall dwell safely: and this is His name by which He shall be called: The Lord Our Righteousness. (Jeremiah 23:6)

Sun of Righteousness: But unto you who revere and worshipfully fear My name shall the Sun of Righteousness arise with healing in His wings and His beams, and you shall go forth and gambol like calves [released] from the stall and leap for joy. (Malachi 4:2)

Strengthener: But when the Comforter (Counselor, Helper, Advocate, Intercessor, Strengthener, Standby) comes, Whom I will send to you from the Father, the Spirit of Truth Who comes (proceeds) from the Father, He [Himself] will testify regarding Me. (John 15: 26)

Standby: But when the Comforter (Counselor, Helper, Advocate, Intercessor, Strengthener, Standby) comes, Whom I will send to you from the

Father, the Spirit of Truth Who comes (proceeds) from the Father, He [Himself] will testify regarding Me. (John 15: 26)

The Steadfast Love: My Steadfast Love and my Fortress, my High Tower and my Deliverer, my Shield and He in Whom I trust and take refuge…… (Psalm 144:2)

My Strength and My Stronghold: Then [Ezra] told them, Go your way, eat the fat, drink the sweet drink, and send portions to him for whom nothing is prepared; for this day is holy to our Lord. And be not grieved and depressed, for the joy of the Lord is your strength and stronghold. (Nehemiah 8:10)

My Surety: Be surety for Your servant for good [as Judah was surety for the safety of Benjamin]; let not the proud oppress me. (Psalm 119: 122)

The Supreme: Let them praise and exalt the name of the Lord, for His name alone is exalted and supreme! His glory and majesty are above earth and heaven! (Psalm 148:13)

The Sufficient One: (Shaddai) Wail, for the day of the Lord is at hand; as destruction from the Almighty and Sufficient One [Shaddai] will it come! (Isaiah 13:6)

My Strong Tower: The name of the Lord is a strong tower; the [consistently] righteous man [upright and in right standing with God] runs into it and is safe, high [above evil] and strong. (Proverbs 18:10)

Our High Tower: The Lord of hosts is with us; the God of Jacob is our Refuge (our Fortress and High Tower). (Psalm 46:7)

Our Teacher: Then Jesus answered him, Blessed (happy, fortunate, and to be envied) are you, Simon Bar-Jonah. For flesh and blood [men] have not revealed this to you, but My Father Who is in heaven. (Matthew 16:17)

It is written in [the book of] the Prophets, And they shall all be taught of God [have Him in person for their Teacher]. Everyone who has listened to and learned from the Father comes to Me (John 6: 45)

And though the Lord gives you the bread of adversity and the water of affliction, yet your Teacher will not hide Himself any more, but your eyes will constantly behold your Teacher (Isaiah 30:20)

A Tested Stone: Therefore thus says the Lord God, Behold, I am laying in Zion for a foundation a Stone, a tested Stone, a precious Cornerstone of sure foundation; he who believes (trusts in, relies on, and adheres to that Stone) will not be ashamed or give way or hasten away [in sudden panic]. (Isaiah 28: 16)

The Truth: Jesus said to him, I am the Way and <u>the Truth</u> and the Life; no one comes to the Father except by (through) Me. (John 14:6)

The God of Truth and Faithfulness: Into Your hands I commit my spirit; You have redeemed me, O Lord, <u>the God of truth and faithfulness</u>. (Psalm 31:5)

The True Vine: <u>I am the True Vine</u>, and My Father is the Vinedresser. (John 15:1)

The Trustworthy Witness: And from Jesus Christ <u>the faithful and trustworthy Witness,</u> the Firstborn of the dead [first to be brought back to life] and the Prince (Ruler) of the kings of the earth. To Him Who ever loves us and has once [for all] loosed and freed us from our sins by His own blood, (Revelation 1:5)

The Spirit of Truth: But when the <u>Comforter</u> (Counselor, Helper, Advocate, Intercessor, Strengthener, Standby) comes, Whom I will send to you from the Father, the Spirit of Truth Who comes (proceeds) from the Father, He [Himself] will testify regarding Me. (John 15: 26)

God of Truth and Faithfulness: So [it shall be] that he who invokes a blessing on himself in the land shall do so by saying, May <u>the God of truth and fidelity</u> [the Amen] bless me; and he who takes an oath in the land shall swear by <u>the God of truth and faithfulness</u> to His promises [the Amen], because the former troubles are forgotten and because they are hidden from My eyes. (Isaiah 65:16)

The Truth-Giving Spirit: But when He, the Spirit of Truth (the Truth-giving Spirit) comes, He will guide you into all the Truth (the whole, full Truth). For He will not speak His own message [on His own authority]; but He will tell whatever He hears [from the Father; He will give the message that has been given to Him], and He will announce and declare to you the things that are to come [that will happen in the future]. (John 16:13)

The Tree of Life: She is a tree of life to those who lay hold on her; and happy (blessed, fortunate, to be envied) is everyone who holds her fast. (Proverbs 3:18)

Our Vindicator: For I know that my Redeemer and Vindicator lives, and at last He [the Last One] will stand upon the earth (Job 19:25)

The Way: Jesus said to him, I am the Way and the Truth and the Life; no one comes to the Father except by (through) Me. (John 14:6)

Our Waymaker: Then Moses stretched out his hand over the sea, and the Lord caused the sea to go back by a strong east wind all that night and made the sea dry land; and the waters were divided (Exodus 14: 21)

God is to us a God of deliverances and salvation; <u>and to God the Lord belongs escape from death [setting us free]</u>.(Psalm 68:20)

Wisdom: <u>I, Wisdom</u> [from God], make prudence my dwelling, and I find out knowledge and discretion. (Proverbs 8:12)

The Wisdom of God: But to those who are called, whether Jew or Greek (Gentile), <u>Christ [is] the Power of God and the Wisdom of God.</u> (1 Corinthians 1:24)

The Word of God: In the beginning [before all-time] was the Word (Christ), and the Word was with God, and <u>the Word was God Himself.</u> (John 1: 1)

Wonderful: This also comes from the Lord of hosts, <u>Who is wonderful</u> in counsel [and] excellent in wisdom and effectual working. (Isaiah 28:29)

Wonderful Counsellor: For to us a Child is born, to us a Son is given; and the government shall be upon His shoulder, and His name shall be called <u>Wonderful Counsellor</u>, Mighty God, Everlasting Father [of Eternity], Prince of Peace. (Isaiah 9:6)

The Builder of Firm Foundations: You laid the foundations of the earth, that it should not be moved forever. (Psalm 104:5)

Yahweh: I appeared to Abraham, to Isaac, and to Jacob as God Almighty [El-Shaddai], but by My name the Lord [Yahweh—the redemptive name of God] I did not make Myself known to them [in acts and great miracles]. (Exodus 6:3)

Giving Thanks Unto The Lord

O give thanks unto the Lord, call upon His name, make known His doings among the peoples!

Sing to Him, sing praises to Him; meditate on and talk of all His marvellous deeds and devoutly praise them.

Glory in His holy name; let the hearts of those rejoice who seek and require the Lord [as their indispensable necessity].

Seek, inquire of and for the Lord, and crave Him and His strength (His might and inflexibility to temptation); seek and require His face and His presence [continually] evermore.

[Earnestly] remember the marvellous deeds that He has done, His miracles and wonders, the judgments and sentences which He pronounced [upon His enemies, as in Egypt].

O you offspring of Abraham His servant, you children of Jacob, His chosen ones,

He is the Lord our God; His judgments are in all the earth.

He is [earnestly] mindful of His covenant and forever it is imprinted on His heart, the word which He commanded and established to a thousand generations,

The covenant which He made with Abraham and His sworn promise to Isaac,

Which He confirmed to Jacob as a statute, to Israel as an everlasting covenant,

Saying, Unto you will I give the land of Canaan as your measured portion, possession, and inheritance.

When they were but a few men in number, in fact, very few, and were temporary residents and strangers in it,

When they went from one nation to another, from one kingdom to another people,

He allowed no man to do them wrong; in fact, He reproved kings for their sakes,

Saying, Touch not My anointed, and do My prophets no harm. (Psalm 105: 1-15)

> **The Name of The Lord is The Gift of His grace and Reward to those who kept His precepts (i.e. hearing; receiving; loving and obeying them) (psalm 119: 56)**

Gods plan for humanity is good and not evil, that is the reason why God reminded us in the book of Jeremiah 23:27 that anything or anyone may create their own idea to confuse people or to plan to negate the promises of God, but God's promises of Blessings stands for those who are conscious of His Name and for those who keeps His precepts.

> **….Who think that they can cause My people to forget My name by their dreams which every man tells to his neighbour, just as their fathers forgot My name because of Baal? (Jeremiah 23:27)**

BOOKS AUTHORED BY FOLAKE HASSAN

The Attributes of God

We All Have Reasons to Praise God

Coming Out of Bondage

The Names of God

God is Good

Becoming a Christian

Becoming a Christian is not a difficult task at all. The Holy Bible instructs every mankind to be born again by confessing our sin and accept Jesus Christ as our Lord and Saviour by praying a simple prayer of salvation.

Prayer of Salvation

Father God, I come to You in the Name of Jesus Christ. According to your Word in the book of Roman 10:9, which says "If you acknowledge and confess with your lips that Jesus is Lord and in your heart believe (adhere to, trusts in, and rely on the truth) that God raised Him from the dead, you will be saved.
I confess Jesus Christ as my Lord and Saviour, Lord Jesus come into my life and forgive me for all my sins. Be Lord of my life in Jesus name, Amen.

Congratulations if you have just prayed this prayer, you are now a Christian and you are saved.

You now have rights to all the promises of God in the Holy Bible.

I will advise you to read the Holy Bible and other Christian literatures regularly to build up your faith in the Lord. Also you will need a Word based church to attend regularly i.e. be part of a good local church that teaches Christian to grow in The Word of God.

*****Please write to us through our website contact page at www.theblessedchristian.co.uk **to inform us of your new decision you made to become a Christian and we will continue to offer all helps necessary for you to grow in Christ.**

Remain Blessed

Yours in Christ

Folake Hassan (Mrs)

Founder/President: The Blessed Christian Centre

About The Author

Folake Hassan is the Owner of The Online Christian Bookshop named The Blessed Christian: www.theblessedchristian.co.uk . She is the Author of the books titled "The Attributes of God" and "Coming Out of Bondage". It is Folake's passion to see souls saved and confess Jesus Christ as their Lord and Saviour. Folake Hassan is blessed with 3 children with the youngest being 18 years of age at the time of writing this book. Folake and her children live in London, United Kingdom.

www.ingramcontent.com/pod-product-compliance
Lightning Source LLC
Chambersburg PA
CBHW020020050426
42450CB00005B/570